# Cooking in the Nude

*For Wine Lovers*

Written by Debbie and Stephen Cornwell
Designed by Carolyn Weary Brandt

Library of Congress Catalog Card Number: 99-71596
ISBN 1-57427-082-6

Printed in Canada
Published by Howell Press, Inc., 1713-2D Allied Lane,
Charlottesville, VA  22903
Telephone: (804) 977-4006
http://www.howellpress.com

First Printing

**HOWELL PRESS**

# TABLE OF CONTENTS

# INTRODUCTION

*C*ooking in the Nude for Wine Lovers is the playful yet passionate approach to pairing impeccable cuisine with excellent wines. Whether you're planning an afternoon of tasteful teasing or an evening of delicious decadence, our romantic recipes are sure to inspire your endeavors.

An apt French proverb says, "Without bread, without wine, love is nothing." *Cooking in the Nude for Wine Lovers* offers you a tantalizing collection of succulent recipes from which to choose and full menu suggestions, including wines! However, an Epicurean sense of humor is a prerequisite to getting complete satisfaction from this book. We encourage you to read each chapter, beginning with "Grape Expectations" (Creating the Mood). Sample "Forbidden Fruits" (A Word on Wines), and after "Popping the Cork" (Appetizers), you'll both be ready to "Zin Now . . . Play Later" (Entrées). Our suggestive titles, like "Nibbling Noir" and "Unquenchable Me," are meant to tempt and tease both you and your dining companion. Only the recipes are serious. They're presented in an easy-to-use format, complete with preparation times.

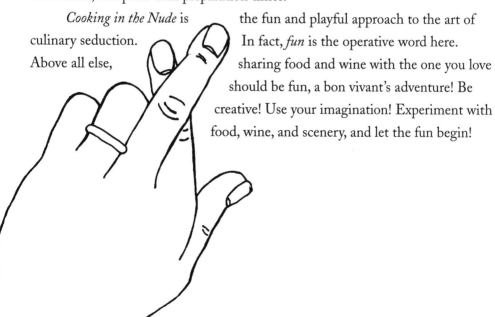

*Cooking in the Nude* is culinary seduction. Above all else, the fun and playful approach to the art of In fact, *fun* is the operative word here. sharing food and wine with the one you love should be fun, a bon vivant's adventure! Be creative! Use your imagination! Experiment with food, wine, and scenery, and let the fun begin!

# *GRAPE EXPECTATIONS*
## (Creating the Mood)

Whether a spontaneous day trip or a first-rate skinny dip, lovers' favorite activities are often heightened, or even instigated, by wine. Wine is actually a form of recreation in and of itself; in fact, it's one of the few diversions that lets us enjoy other leisure activities simultaneously. Most importantly, wine enhances all of the pastimes that lovers can dream of or engage in. For example, the classic picnic was invented by Omar Khayyám, who wooed with, "A loaf of bread, a jug of wine, and thou."

Just as a good wine is born of experimentation and imagination coupled with nurturing, so is a satisfying love life. Take time to do special little things, plan surprises, and relish the moments! Try new adventures and share meals and wine, for, as the wise philosopher Euripides once said, "Where there is no wine, there is no love." We'd like to suggest six fantasy vignettes to stimulate the bon vivant in anyone.

Surprise the love of your life with a "Gamay Getaway." Whether it's a sudden whim or a special occasion, grab a great bottle of wine and the car keys and go. A weekend away is a wonderful way to shut out the world and get reacquainted with your lover. "Now and Zin" it's nice to be alone!

Or, sip into something more comfortable after a day of skiing. Sharing a crisp Sauvignon Blanc by the fireplace is the perfect way to end a day—and begin an evening of playful romance. Later, perhaps a little Champagne and a bubble bath for two . . . But remember, those tiny bubbles can be dangerous!

If it's warm outside, you might just like to "Take a Chance" on alfresco romance. Pack up the umbrellas, towels, lotion, and a bottle of chilled Riesling and head for the beach. While sipping, trade fantasies about sailing away to a deserted tropical isle. On the way home, suggest a light supper and a little dip in the hot tub, au naturel, accompanied by a spicy Gewürztraminer . . . naturally.

Almost as easily, you could surprise your special someone with tickets to the new play that everyone is raving about. Present the tickets along with two luscious, buttery glasses of Chardonnay. Afterward, a late night supper with

Champagne, and for dessert ... Well, how you conclude the evening will be left totally to your imagination!

It's a crisp, cool fall day, all the leaves are changing color, and your lover is restless. It's too beautiful to be indoors ... Suggest a day of wine tasting! Pack a few hors d'oeuvres, a couple of glasses, a big blanket, and a few CDs. After tasting at several wineries, select a wine you both love. Then find a grassy knoll for your picnic. Once the wine and goodies have been shared and the music has you both relaxed, hint at your inclination to give a light massage. But, take heed—"A Wink and a Drink" may lead to more than you think!

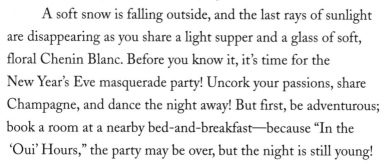

A soft snow is falling outside, and the last rays of sunlight are disappearing as you share a light supper and a glass of soft, floral Chenin Blanc. Before you know it, it's time for the New Year's Eve masquerade party! Uncork your passions, share Champagne, and dance the night away! But first, be adventurous; book a room at a nearby bed-and-breakfast—because "In the 'Oui' Hours," the party may be over, but the night is still young!

# FORBIDDEN FRUITS
## (A Word on Wines)

*S*oft and supple, lean and leggy, glamorous and graceful, bold and intense, fresh and lively . . . Love, like wine, comes in many flavors. Which noble wine will bring you and your true love to an outrageously romantic evening's end? Here's a primer on the tantalizing tastes in the creative lover's cellar.

### White Wines

**Chenin Blanc*** is as charming as it is versatile. A light, fresh, and flowery white wine, it's available in both a dry and a sweet style. Both versions complement fish, seafood, chicken, and salads and are particularly good with spicy fare, ham, or other smoked meats.

**Riesling** is an elegantly fresh, light, floral wine and is available in a range of dry to sweet. A chameleon-like wine that seems to go well with almost everything, it is delicious with spicy or salty foods, hot or cold hors d'oeuvres, and salads. It is an especially good counterpart to fish or seafood with light or creamy sauces. Served well-chilled in the summer, Riesling is the quintessential "patio wine."

**Gewürztraminer** is a particularly spicy, fruity wine. It is well suited to Asian foods, curries, and grilled or broiled chicken or fish. Hearty sausages and spicy foods or sauces also pair well with this wine, which is available in versions ranging from the very dry to the very sweet.

**Sauvignon Blanc*** is a true classic, a fresh, soft, dry white wine that can be variously described as crisp, grassy, fruity, or citrusy in flavor. Highly complementary to delicate or light sauces, it goes well with most foods and is especially delightful with seafood (like scallops, prawns, and crab), hearty flavors (garlic or pesto sauces), and delicate risottos. When in doubt, Sauvignon Blanc is always a good choice.

*Popular wines that are a sure bet. Consult your local wine merchant for specific recommendations.

**Chardonnay\*** is a gracefully rounded wine. Its luscious flavors can run from apple and pear to oak and butter. Its rich, silky characteristics make it an unsurpassed accompaniment to salmon, crab, and elegant cream sauces. Pair it with almost any dish for excellent results; seafood, chicken, pork, and even beef find a good match in Chardonnay.

**Pinot Blanc\*** is very similar to Chardonnay, with slightly less intensity. It enhances most meals but is particularly good with fish, seafood, and chicken dishes with simple sauces.

**Pinot Grigio**, or **Pinot Gris**, is a full-bodied wine. Its spicy characteristics make it an ideal counterpart to boldly flavored dishes like tangy barbecued fish or chicken or hearty salads.

**Champagne**, or **sparkling wine**, is available in a range of very dry to very sweet. The driest is Extra Brut. Brut is the next driest and is followed by Extra Dry (which isn't). Sec is a wee bit sweet, Demi-Sec is definitely sweet, and Doux is very sweet. We prefer the Extra Brut or Brut, which complement a variety of hors d'oeuvres and light chicken or fish dishes with delicate sauces. Seafood— particularly lobster, crab, prawns, scallops, cold salmon, and chilled seafood salads—is especially good when paired with Champagne or sparkling wine.

## Red Wines

**Pinot Noir** is a smooth, fragrant, full-bodied wine with spicy overtones. It is a fine wine to serve with lamb, pork, and beef, especially when those dishes are served with rich sauces.

**Gamay Beaujolais**, a lighter wine than Pinot Noir, is soft, rounded, and subtle, with a fresh fruity flavor. It goes well with rich, full-flavored dishes, like pork chops and spicy pastas. It complements light dishes as well. Consider pairing it with salads or hors d'oeuvres.

**Cabernet Sauvignon\*** is the king of red wines. Rich, big, and bold, with flavors of cassis and berries, it is an elegant dry wine that enhances filets mignons and steaks, particularly those with rich sauces. It is especially complementary to a variety of cheeses, such as Gorgonzola and Camembert. For a truly sensual experience, pair it with dark chocolate.

**Merlot**\* is similar to but lighter than Cabernet Sauvignon. Soft, velvety, plummy, and sometimes peppery, it's a fine choice to accompany veal, chicken, salmon, and pasta. It is also very good in combination with squash, spinach, roasted vegetables, or roasted garlic.

**Zinfandel**\* is unique. As a young wine, it can be full and fresh, with flavors of raspberry and blackberry. As such, it is an excellent choice with pastas, shellfish stews, or sausages. A young Zinfandel is also a good match for bold, spicy fare or dishes that include cheese or grilled peppers. As an older wine, Zinfandel develops elegant, rich, rustic flavors that are sometimes peppery or earthy. At this stage it beautifully complements grilled lamb, beef, and wild fowl, like duck or quail.

**Petite Sirah** is known for its full body and depth. It is a robust, peppery wine that enhances big, boldly flavored dishes like steaks, prime rib, or barbecued ribs.

**Barbera** is a full-bodied and hearty wine that has a sharpness that is both pleasing and well suited to tomato pastas, spicy sauces, sausages, and grilled beef.

# PRIVATE RESERVE
## (The Well-Stocked Pantry)

| | | |
|---|---|---|
| Almonds | Dried cranberries | Rice, arborio |
| Angel hair pasta | Fennel seeds | Rice, white |
| Apple cider | Fettuccine | Rosemary |
| Apple cider vinegar | Fines herbes | Rum |
| Arrowroot | Flour, all-purpose | Saffron |
| Artichokes, canned | Honey | Sage |
| Baby clams, whole, canned | Ketchup | Salt |
| Basil | Kirsch | Savory |
| Beef stock | Lasagna | Seasoned salt |
| Black cherries, canned | Lemon zest | Sherry |
| Black olives, canned, | Linguine | Soy sauce, light |
| sliced | Mace | Spinach, chopped and |
| Brandy | Madeira | frozen |
| Bread crumbs | Marjoram | Sugar |
| Brown sugar | Marsala | Tarragon |
| Calvados | Mustard, Dijon | Thyme |
| Capers | Nutmeg | Tomato paste |
| Cayenne | Olive oil | Tomato sauce |
| Celery salt | Olive oil, light | Tomatoes, canned, diced, |
| Chervil | Oregano | and peeled |
| Chicken stock | Paprika | Tortellini |
| Chicken stock, low-salt | Parsley | Turmeric |
| Chili powder | Pâté de fois gras, canned | Vegetable broth |
| Chilies, diced and canned | Pepper | Vegetable oil |
| Chives | Pernod | Vermouth |
| Cilantro | Petite peas, frozen | Walnuts |
| Clam juice, bottled | Poppy seeds | White beans, small, canned |
| Corn, canned | Port wine | White pepper |
| Cornstarch | Raisins | White wine, dry (e.g., |
| Cumin | Red wine, dry (e.g., | Chardonnay, Chenin |
| Curry powder | Burgundy, Zinfandel) | Blanc, Sauternes) |
| Dill | Red wine vinegar | Worcestershire sauce |

# Phyllo Stuffed with Spinach and Cheese   1 hour

**Step One:**

1 Tbsp. butter
1/4 cup minced green onions
1 10-oz. package frozen chopped
   spinach, thawed and squeezed dry
1/3 cup feta cheese
1/3 cup minced parsley
1/4 tsp. dill
1 egg, beaten
salt and pepper to taste

Melt butter in frying pan over medium heat and sauté green onions until tender. Mix in spinach and move to a bowl. Add feta, parsley, and dill; mix well. Blend in egg, salt, and pepper.

**Step Two:**

1/2 cup butter, melted
1 package phyllo leaves

Preheat oven to 425° and lightly butter baking sheet. Cut one phyllo leaf into strips 2" wide and brush with butter. Work with one strip at a time; keep others moist under sheet of wax paper topped with a damp towel. Place a teaspoon of filling on end of leaf and fold repeatedly to form a triangle. Brush with butter and place on baking sheet. Repeat with remaining phyllo strips, working quickly. Brush all triangles with butter and bake 15 minutes.

**Step Three:**

fresh dill sprigs
cherry tomatoes

Arrange triangles on serving tray and garnish with dill and tomatoes. Serve hot.

# Gruyère Cheese Puffs

1 hour

**Step One:**

1 cup all-purpose flour
3/4 tsp. salt
1/2 tsp. freshly ground pepper
1/2 tsp. thyme
pinch cayenne

Preheat oven to 425°. Combine flour, salt, pepper, thyme, and cayenne in a bowl; set aside.

**Step Two:**

1 cup milk
1/2 cup butter

In large saucepan, bring milk and butter to a boil, stirring often. Remove from heat and add flour mixture all at once. Using a wooden spoon, stir briskly until dough forms a ball and comes away from sides of pan. Remove to bowl.

**Step Three:**

5 large eggs
6 oz. freshly grated Parmesan cheese
1/2 cup freshly grated Gruyère cheese

Using mixer, beat eggs into dough one at a time until well blended. Add cheeses and stir by hand until well blended. Spoon 1" balls of dough onto greased baking sheet 2 inches apart. (Or, use pastry bag with star tip.) Bake 10 minutes or until golden brown; serve warm.

# Salmon-Caviar Rolls

20 minutes

**Step One:**

4 oz. cream cheese
2 Tbsp. sour cream
1 oz. red caviar

Blend cream cheese and sour cream together until smooth. Fold in caviar.

**Step Two:**

4 oz. smoked salmon, thinly sliced
parsley sprigs
1/2 lemon, cut into wedges

Spread cream cheese mixture onto salmon slices; roll up and cut into servings 1" wide. Arrange on small platter and garnish with parsley and lemon wedges. Chill until ready to serve.

# Artichoke Dip

**40 minutes**

1/2 cup mayonnaise
1/2 cup grated Cheddar cheese
1/2 cup freshly grated Parmesan cheese
1 small can diced chilies
1 8-oz. can artichokes, chopped

Preheat oven to 350°. Combine all ingredients in an ovenproof bowl; mix thoroughly. Bake for 25 minutes. Serve with crackers or bite-size cubes of French bread.


# Herbed Wine and Cheese Spread

**30 minutes**
(chill 1 hour)

**Step One:**
1/4 lb. Monterey Jack cheese, grated
1 8-oz. package cream cheese
1 1/2 oz. Parmesan cheese, grated

In bowl, soften cream cheese with a fork. Add other cheeses and mix well.

**Step Two:**
1/4 tsp. marjoram
1/4 tsp. dill
1/4 tsp. seasoned salt
1 1/2 Tbsp. softened butter
1/4 cup Chenin Blanc

Fold herbs, seasoning, and butter into cheese mixture. Blend in wine until smooth. Spoon into crock or serving bowl and chill at least 1 hour. Serve with crackers.

# Basil-Scented Sweet Potato Soup

**1 hour, 30 minutes**

**Step One:**

3 small sweet potatoes

Prick sweet potatoes with fork. Place in a baking dish and bake 1 hour at 400°.

**Step Two:**

1/2 cup sliced leeks
2 cups chicken broth
1/4 cup whipping cream
1 tsp. Marsala
2 Tbsp. freshly minced basil
pinch cayenne
2 Tbsp. sour cream
parsley sprigs

Combine leeks and chicken broth in saucepan over medium heat and simmer until leeks are tender. Pour into food processor. Scoop sweet potatoes from skins; add to processor and puree until smooth. Return to pan and bring to a boil. Reduce heat and add cream, Marsala, basil, and cayenne. Simmer 5 minutes. Ladle into small bowls and garnish with parsley and a dollop of sour cream.

# Woodsy Madeira-Mushroom Soup

**2 hours**

**Step One:**

4 Tbsp. butter
1 yellow onion, finely chopped
1 lb. fresh crimini or white mushrooms, thinly sliced
1/2 tsp. thyme
salt and freshly ground pepper to taste
4 cups chicken stock

In stockpot, melt butter over medium heat. Add onions and sauté until lightly browned. Add mushrooms; cook until they begin to give up their juices. Season with thyme, salt, and pepper. Add chicken stock. Cover, turn heat to low, and simmer 45 minutes.

**Step Two:**

1–2 Tbsp. Madeira
parsley sprigs

Using a slotted spoon, transfer onions and mushrooms to food processor along with 1 cup of broth. Process until smooth. Return puree to stockpot, turn heat to medium, and add Madeira to taste. Simmer 5 minutes. Ladle into bowls, garnish with a sprig of fresh parsley, and serve.

# Avocados Stuffed with Tomatoes, Feta, and Chives

**1 hour, 20 minutes**

**Step One:**

1/2 cucumber, peeled, seeded, and chopped
2 Roma tomatoes, chopped
2 Tbsp. snipped chives
2 Tbsp. freshly minced parsley
3 oz. feta cheese
1/2 tsp. dill
1 1/2 Tbsp. light olive oil
1 Tbsp. red wine vinegar

Combine all ingredients in a bowl and chill in refrigerator for 45 minutes to an hour.

**Step Two:**

1 large avocado, peeled, halved, and pitted
2 large lettuce leaves

Place each lettuce leaf on a plate and top with avocado half. Fill cavity with chilled mixture, spilling some onto lettuce leaf. Serve.

# Kiwi, Orange, and Cranberry Salad with Poppy Seed Dressing

**20 minutes**

**Step One:**

2 navel oranges, peeled
3 kiwi, peeled
1/3 cup dried cranberries

Lay oranges on their sides and cut into 1/4" slices, then into bite-size pieces. Halve kiwi lengthwise. Cut crosswise into slices. Put kiwi, oranges, and cranberries in a bowl.

**Step Two:**

1 cup plain yogurt
1 Tbsp. honey
1 Tbsp. freshly squeezed lemon juice
1/2 tsp. poppy seeds

Mix yogurt, honey, and lemon juice; taste and adjust. Stir in poppy seeds.

**Step Three:**

red or butter leaf lettuce

Arrange lettuce on salad plates and spoon fruit onto leaves. Drizzle with dressing and serve.

# Tomato-Olive Salad with Cumin-Scented Dressing

**15 minutes**

(marinate 1 hour)

**Step One:**

4 Roma tomatoes, cut into wedges

1 cup black olives

4 oz. Monterey Jack cheese, cut into
   1/2" cubes

2 Tbsp. snipped chives

2 Tbsp. finely chopped parsley

Combine ingredients in a bowl.

**Step Two:**

4 Tbsp. freshly squeezed lemon juice

6 Tbsp. olive oil

2 tsp. sugar

1 tsp. salt

3/4 tsp. cumin

1/8 tsp. turmeric

pinch saffron

freshly ground pepper to taste

1/2 lb. mixed greens (e.g., arugula,
   radicchio, red leaf, romaine, endive)

Combine marinade ingredients and toss with tomato-olive mixture; cover and chill for 1 hour. Arrange mixed greens on salad plates. Spoon marinated vegetables over greens and serve.

## ♥ Nibbling Noir

45 minutes

*I've got the grapes, if you've got the time . . .*

Veal Chops and Mushrooms in Madeira-Herb Sauce

**Step One:**

1/4 cup flour
salt and pepper to taste
4 boneless veal loin chops
3 Tbsp. butter
1 Tbsp. light olive oil

Put flour, salt, and pepper in a large plastic bag. Add veal and shake to coat. In frying pan over medium heat, melt butter and oil. Add chops and brown on both sides. Transfer to a warm plate.

**Step Two:**

1/2 cup minced onion
1 clove garlic, minced
8–10 mushrooms, sliced
1/2 cup Madeira
1/2 cup beef broth
2 tsp. tomato paste
1/4 tsp. marjoram
1/2 tsp. thyme
1/2 tsp. sage
1 bay leaf

Add onions and garlic to pan and sauté until onion softens. Add mushrooms and continue to sauté 6–7 minutes. Add Madeira and bring to a boil. Boil 1–2 minutes. Add remaining ingredients and return to a boil. Reduce heat to low; return veal to pan and simmer 10–12 minutes. Transfer veal and mushrooms to warm au gratin dishes or plates and keep warm.

**Step Three:**

3 Tbsp. butter, cut into pieces
2 Tbsp. minced parsley

Skim fat from liquid. Turn heat to high and boil until sauce thickens slightly. Whisk in butter, one piece at a time. Spoon sauce over veal and garnish with parsley.

## SUGGESTED MENU

Popping the Cork

*Phyllo Stuffed with Spinach and Cheese*

Riesling to the Occasion

*Kiwi, Orange, and Cranberry Salad with Poppy Seed Dressing*

Zin Now . . . Play Later

♥ *Nibbling Noir*

Peel Me a Grape

*Julienne of Carrots and Parsnips with Rosemary*

Forbidden Fruit

*Pinot Noir*

# ♥ Merlot Mischief

45 minutes

*Memoirs are made of this!*

Veal Chops in Brandied Walnut Sauce

**Step One:**
3/4 cup walnuts

Using blender or food processor, convert walnuts into a paste.

**Step Two:**
4 boneless veal loin chops
salt and pepper to taste
2 Tbsp. butter

Pat veal dry and season both sides with salt and pepper. Melt butter in frying pan over medium heat. Add veal and brown lightly, about 3 minutes per side. Remove chops to warm plates; cover and keep warm.

**Step Three:**
1/2 cup Sauternes or other dry white wine
1/2 cup whipping cream
1/2 cup beef broth
1/4 cup brandy

Pour fat from pan. Add wine and bring to a boil, stirring up brown bits from the pan's bottom. Boil 2–3 minutes or until liquid is reduced to a glaze. Blend in cream, broth, and brandy. Return to a boil and boil until liquid is reduced by half. Reduce heat to low and whisk in 3 Tbsp. of walnut paste.

**Step Four:**
1/4 cup walnut halves
1 Tbsp. snipped chives

Spoon sauce over veal. Garnish with walnuts, sprinkle with chives, and serve.

22

## SUGGESTED MENU

Popping the Cork

*Phyllo Stuffed with Spinach and Cheese*

Riesling to the Occasion

*Woodsy Madeira-Mushroom Soup*

*Kiwi, Orange, and Cranberry Salad*

*with Poppy Seed Dressing*

Zin Now . . . Play Later

*Merlot Mischief*

Peel Me a Grape

*Gratin of Spinach, Zucchini, and Herbs*

Forbidden Fruit

*Merlot*

# Wine Not?!

*I have a crush on you!*

## Rib Eye Steaks in Wine Sauce with Oranges

**Step One:**

1 Tbsp. vegetable oil
1 onion, chopped
1/2 carrot, chopped
3/4 cup beef broth
1 cup water
3 Tbsp. chopped parsley
1 bay leaf
1/4 tsp. thyme
2 tsp. arrowroot dissolved in 4 tsp.
   cold water

Heat oil in frying pan over medium heat. Add onion and carrot and sauté 5–8 minutes. Add remaining ingredients except arrowroot blend. Reduce heat to low and simmer 20 minutes. Strain liquid from vegetables and return liquid to pan. Skim off fat and boil until reduced to 1 cup. Turn heat to medium, whisk in arrowroot mixture, and cook until sauce thickens. Set aside.

**Step Two:**

1 Tbsp. vegetable oil
2 rib eye steaks, boned and pounded
   to 1/3" thickness
3/4 cup Zinfandel or other dry red wine
1/3 cup minced onion
1/4 tsp. thyme
1 bay leaf

Heat oil in frying pan over medium-high heat and cook steaks, turning often, to desired doneness. Remove to warm plate; cover and keep warm. Remove fat from frying pan, add wine, and turn heat to high. Add remaining ingredients and boil until reduced to 1/4 cup.

**Step Three:**

2 Tbsp. butter
1 orange, peeled and divided into
   segments

In small frying pan, melt butter over medium heat. Add oranges and sauté 3–4 minutes. Set aside.

**Step Four:**

2 Tbsp. butter
2 tsp. snipped chives
1 Tbsp. minced parsley
1/2 tsp. tarragon
pinch of sugar
parsley sprigs

Strain wine sauce from Step 2 into sauce from Step 1, removing bay leaf. Boil until slightly thickened. Reduce heat to low, whisk in butter, and add remaining ingredients. Spoon sauce over steaks, garnish with oranges and parsley sprigs, and serve.

# SUGGESTED MENU

Popping the Cork

*Artichoke Dip*

Riesling to the Occasion

*Avocados Stuffed with Tomatoes, Feta, and Chives*

Zin Now . . . Play Later

*Wine Not?!*

Peel Me a Grape

*Cauliflower in Creamy Basil Sauce*

Forbidden Fruit

*Petite Sirah*

# In Vino Veritas

*In wine there is truth, and the truth is . . . I want you!*

Filets Mignons with Pâté and Herbed Wine Sauce

**Step One:**

| | |
|---|---|
| 1 Tbsp. butter | Preheat oven to 350°. Melt butter in frying |
| 1 slice bacon, diced | pan over medium heat. Sauté bacon and onion |
| 3 Tbsp. minced onion | until bacon is done. Add flour, whisking |
| 1 Tbsp. flour | constantly for 2 minutes. Add ketchup, |
| 1 tsp. ketchup | mushrooms, stock, wine, salt, and pepper. |
| 4 mushrooms, chopped | Bring to a boil; turn heat to low and simmer |
| 3/4 cup beef stock | 15 minutes. Add herbs and simmer 2–3 |
| 1/4 cup Zinfandel or other dry | minutes more. Strain through a sieve into |
|    red wine | warm serving dish. Keep warm. |
| salt and pepper to taste | |
| 1 Tbsp. minced parsley | |
| 1/2 tsp. thyme | |
| 1/2 tsp. marjoram | |

**Step Two:**

| | |
|---|---|
| 1 1/2 Tbsp. butter | Put mushroom caps in buttered dish. Dot |
| 4 mushroom caps | with remaining butter and season. Bake for 8– |
| salt and pepper to taste | 10 minutes. |

**Step Three:**

| | |
|---|---|
| 2 filets mignons 1"–2" thick | Barbecue filets or brush with melted butter |
| 1 can pâté de foie gras | and broil 5–8 minutes per side. Remove to |
| parsley sprigs | warm au gratin dishes or plates and top each |
| | with a slice of pâté and 2 mushroom caps. |
| | Spoon sauce over fillets, garnish with parsley, |
| | and serve. |

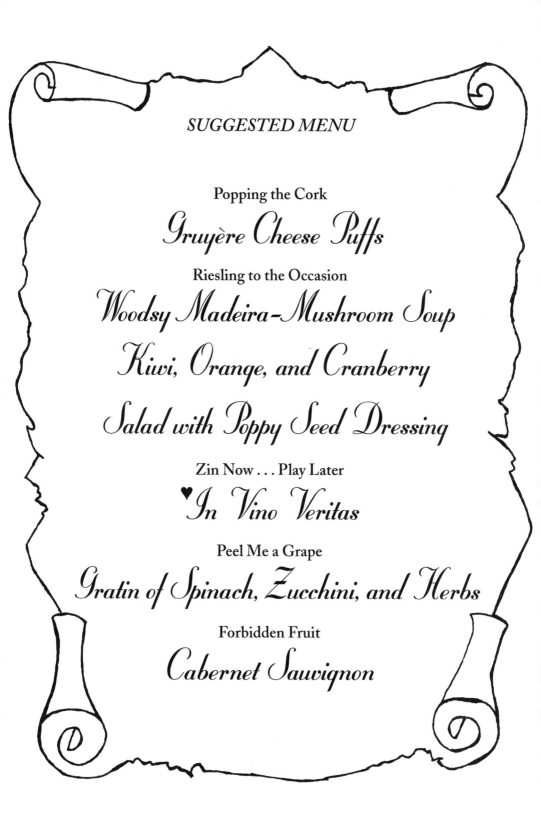

## SUGGESTED MENU

Popping the Cork
### Gruyère Cheese Puffs

Riesling to the Occasion
### Woodsy Madeira–Mushroom Soup

### Kiwi, Orange, and Cranberry

### Salad with Poppy Seed Dressing

Zin Now . . . Play Later
### ♥In Vino Veritas

Peel Me a Grape
### Gratin of Spinach, Zucchini, and Herbs

Forbidden Fruit
### Cabernet Sauvignon

# Take a Chance

 **1 hour, 30 minutes** 

*On romance, wine not?*

Curried Chicken with Peppers, Raisins, and Almonds

**Step One:**

1/4 cup flour
1 1/2 lbs. chicken pieces
3 Tbsp. vegetable oil
1 onion, chopped
1 clove garlic, chopped
1 green bell pepper, halved and seeded
1 red bell pepper, halved and seeded

Shake flour and chicken in plastic bag until chicken is coated. Heat oil in frying pan over medium heat. Add chicken and brown on all sides. Remove. Sauté onion, garlic, and peppers in frying pan until tender.

**Step Two:**

2 tsp. curry powder
1/2 tsp. salt
freshly ground pepper to taste
1/4 tsp. mace
1 1-lb. can diced, peeled tomatoes
1/2 cup Sauternes or other dry white
    wine
2 Tbsp. chopped parsley
1/3 cup raisins

Drain excess vegetable oil from frying pan. Add curry powder, salt, pepper, and mace and cook 1 minute. Add remaining ingredients and reduce heat to low. Return chicken to pan and simmer, covered, for 40 minutes. Meanwhile, begin Step Three.

**Step Three:**

1 1/2 cups uncooked rice
1/4 cup slivered almonds, toasted in
    dry pan

Cook rice according to package directions. Divide onto warm plates, top with chicken and a spoonful of sauce, garnish with almonds, and serve.

Popping the Cork

## Gruyère Cheese Puffs

Riesling to the Occasion

## Tomato-Olive Salad with Cumin-Scented Dressing

Zin Now . . . Play Later

## Take a Chance

Peel Me a Grape

## Acorn Squash with Bacon

Forbidden Fruit

## Riesling

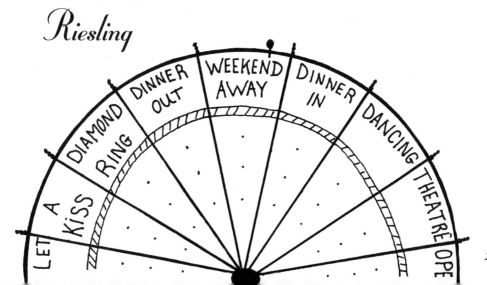

# Blanc Cheque

*Tonight I'm inviting* you *to call the shots!*

Chicken in Tawny Port Wine Cream Sauce

**Step One:**

2 Tbsp. vegetable oil
2 Tbsp. butter
1 onion, thinly sliced
2 boneless, skinless chicken breasts
salt and pepper to taste

In large frying pan over medium heat, sauté onion in oil and butter until brown. Add chicken and sauté 4–5 minutes on each side, until browned; no pink should remain on inside. Season with salt and pepper. Remove chicken to warm plate; cover and keep warm.

**Step Two:**

4 cloves garlic, minced
1 cup tawny Port wine
1/2 cup whipping cream
2 Tbsp. chopped parsley

Add garlic to frying pan and sauté 1 minute. Add Port and bring to a boil, cooking until liquid is reduced by half. Add cream and return to a boil, boiling until sauce thickens slightly. Slice chicken breasts diagonally, into slices 1/2" wide; nap with sauce, garnish with fresh parsley, and serve.

# SUGGESTED MENU

Popping the Cork

*Herbed Wine and Cheese Spread*

Riesling to the Occasion

*Kiwi, Orange, and Cranberry Salad with*

*Poppy Seed Dressing*

Zin Now . . . Play Later

*Blanc Cheque*

Peel Me a Grape

*Gratin of Spinach, Zucchini, and*

*Herbs*

Forbidden Fruit

*Pinot Blanc*

 # Just in Case

*. . . you have a naughty idea, I have a nice bottle of wine!*

Succulent Mushroom Risotto with Grilled Chicken Breasts

**Step One:**

2 Tbsp. butter
1 small onion, finely chopped
1 cup chopped crimini or white
  mushrooms
2 cups Arborio rice
2 cups chicken stock
1 cup Sauternes or other dry white wine

Preheat oven to 400°. In ovenproof saucepan, sauté onion in butter until lightly browned. Add mushrooms and continue to sauté until just tender. Remove to a bowl. Add rice to pan. Stir, toasting rice for 3–5 minutes. Add stock and wine and bring to a boil. Turn heat off. Cover pan and bake in oven 15 minutes or until rice is tender.

**Step Two:**

1/4 cup whipping cream
1/2 cup grated Asiago or Parmesan
  cheese
salt and pepper to taste
5 Roma tomatoes, chopped
5 Tbsp. butter

Transfer rice to frying pan. Add cream and cook until heated through. Mix in cheese and season generously. Add tomatoes and simmer 4–5 minutes. Add butter 1 Tbsp. at a time over residual heat.

**Step Three:**

2 boneless, skinless chicken breasts
oil
salt and pepper to taste
2 tsp. chives

Brush chicken with oil and season with salt and pepper. Grill 3–5 minutes per side or until springy to the touch. Garnish with a sprinkle of chives and serve with risotto on warm plates.

# SUGGESTED MENU

Popping the Cork

## Salmon-Caviar Rolls

Riesling to the Occasion

## Woodsy Madeira-Mushroom Soup

## Avocados Stuffed with Tomatoes, Feta, and Chives

Zin Now . . . Play Later

## ♥Just in Case

Peel Me a Grape

## French White and Green Beans

Forbidden Fruit

## Chardonnay

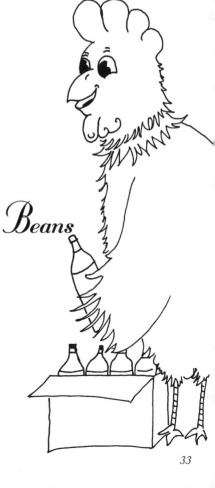

# *Virtuous Vintage*

*Never decline fruit of the vine. It makes your evening really d'vine!*

Crab-Stuffed Chicken in White Wine Sauce

**Step One:**

2 Tbsp. butter
6 large mushrooms, sliced
2 Tbsp. flour
salt and pepper to taste
1/4 cup milk
1/4 lb. fresh crabmeat
1/3 cup grated Swiss cheese

Melt butter in frying pan over medium heat. Sauté mushrooms until tender and moisture has evaporated, about 8–10 minutes. Whisk in flour, salt, and pepper; cook 2 minutes. Whisk in milk until smooth. Add crabmeat and cheese and blend well.

**Step Two:**

2 boneless, skinless chicken breasts, pounded to 1/4" thickness

Spread crab mixture on breasts. Roll up and secure with string or toothpicks.

**Step Three:**

3 Tbsp. flour
1/2 tsp. paprika
1/4 tsp. salt
2 Tbsp. butter
1/2 cup Sauternes or other dry white wine

Combine flour, paprika, and salt; roll chicken in seasoned flour to coat evenly. Melt butter in frying pan over medium heat. Add chicken and brown on all sides. Add wine to pan and reduce heat; cover and simmer 15–20 minutes. Remove chicken to warmed au gratin dishes or dinner plates.

**Step Four:**

2 Tbsp. flour
1 Tbsp. water
2 tsp. freshly grated lemon peel

Blend flour and water in small jar and whisk into liquid remaining from Step Three. Continue to whisk until sauce thickens. Spoon sauce over chicken and garnish with lemon peel.

# SUGGESTED MENU

Popping the Cork

## Phyllo Stuffed with Spinach and Cheese

Riesling to the Occasion

## Woodsy Madeira–Mushroom Soup

## Kiwi, Orange, and Cranberry Salad with

## Poppy Seed Dressing

Zin Now . . . Play Later

## Virtuous Vintage

Peel Me a Grape

## French White and Green Beans

Forbidden Fruit

## Chenin Blanc

 **Rhône Romp**

*Bottoms up!*

Grilled Chicken Breasts in Creamy Tomato-Jalapeño Sauce

**Step One:**

1 jalapeño pepper, halved and seeded

Roast jalapeño over open flame or under broiler until skin blisters. Place in paper bag and close top tightly; steam 10 minutes. Remove charred portions and mince.

**Step Two:**

1/2 onion, finely chopped
3 Tbsp. finely chopped cilantro
1 cup whipping cream
1/2 cup Sauternes or other dry white wine
1 can diced tomatoes, drained
salt and pepper to taste

Combine jalapeño, onion, cilantro, cream, and wine in frying pan. Turn heat to high and boil until sauce is reduced by half. Add tomatoes, salt, and pepper. Turn heat to low and keep warm.

**Step Three:**

2 Tbsp. butter
1 Tbsp. Sauternes or other dry white wine
2 boneless, skinless chicken breasts
cilantro sprigs

Combine butter and wine in a small dish and brush onto chicken. Grill breasts 3–5 minutes per side or until springy to the touch. Transfer to warmed plates, top with sauce, and garnish with cilantro.

# SUGGESTED MENU

Popping the Cork

## Artichoke Dip

Riesling to the Occasion

## Tomato-Olive Salad with Cumin-Scented Dressing

Zin Now . . . Play Later

## Rhône Romp

Peel Me a Grape

## Gratin of Spinach, Zucchini, and Herbs

Forbidden Fruit

## Gamay Beaujolais

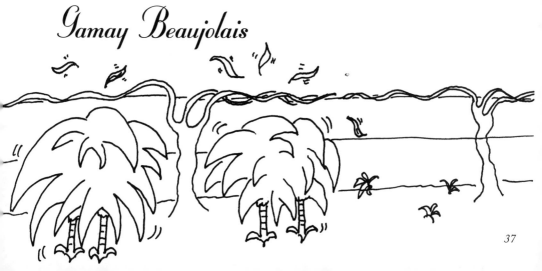

# Raucous Bacchus

*I've got the bubbly . . . Let's party!*

Grilled Chicken Breasts with Citrus Sin-sation Marinade

**Step One:**

1/2 cup sour cream
2 Tbsp. light olive oil
2 Tbsp. freshly squeezed lime juice
2 Tbsp. freshly squeezed orange juice
2 Tbsp. freshly squeezed lemon juice
1 Tbsp. chili powder
1 Tbsp. paprika
1/2 tsp. cayenne
salt and freshly ground pepper to taste

Combine ingredients in food processor or blender and mix until smooth.

**Step Two:**

2 boneless, skinless chicken breasts

Spoon some marinade into glass baking dish. Add chicken in single layer, top with remaining marinade, and chill 3–4 hours.

**Step Three:**

Grill chicken breasts 3–5 minutes per side, or until springy to touch. Serve immediately on warm plates.

# SUGGESTED MENU

Popping the Cork

*Gruyère Cheese Puffs*

Riesling to the Occasion

*Basil-Scented Sweet Potato Soup*

*Tomato-Olive Salad with Cumin-Scented Dressing*

Zin Now ... Play Later

*Raucous Bacchus*

Peel Me a Grape

*Angel Hair Pasta in Herb-Wine Sauce*

Forbidden Fruit

*Chenin Blanc*

# ♥ Splish Splash!

*A champagne bath? My tub bubbles over for you!*

Sautéed Chicken and Vegetables in Pernod Sauce

**Step One:**

1 Tbsp. butter
1 carrot, cut into matchsticks
1 celery stalk, cut into matchsticks
3 green onions, sliced

Melt butter in frying pan over medium heat. Add vegetables and sauté until tender. Remove vegetables to warm plate; cover and keep warm.

**Step Two:**

2 boneless, skinless chicken breasts
salt and pepper to taste
3/4 cup Sauternes or other dry white
  wine
1/3 cup Sherry
2 Tbsp. Pernod
1 bay leaf

Season breasts with salt and pepper and place in frying pan. Add remaining ingredients; cover and simmer 6–8 minutes. Transfer breasts to plate with vegetables.

**Step Three:**

1/2 tsp. basil
1/2 tsp. tarragon
1/2 tsp. thyme
1 tsp. freshly minced lemon peel
4–5 fennel seeds
1/2 cup whipping cream

Add herbs, lemon peel, and fennel seeds to frying pan. Boil until liquid is reduced by half, about 5 minutes. Add cream and liquid from vegetable plate; boil until sauce thickens. Spoon over chicken and vegetables and serve.

# SUGGESTED MENU

Popping the Cork

## *Phyllo Stuffed with Spinach and Cheese*

Riesling to the Occasion

## *Avocados Stuffed with Tomatoes, Feta, and Chives*

Zin Now . . . Play Later

## ♥*Splish Splash!*

Peel Me a Grape

## *Julienne of Carrots and Parsnips with Rosemary*

Forbidden Fruit

## *Champagne or Chenin Blanc*

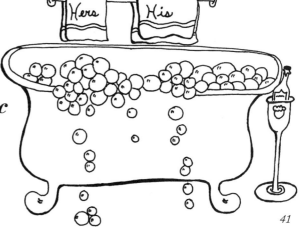

# Over a Barrel

*. . . is where your love leaves me. Let the good times roll!*

Succulent Crab and Spinach Lasagne

**Step One:**

1/2 lb. crimini or white mushrooms, sliced
1/4 cup butter
1/4 cup chopped onion
1 clove garlic, minced
2 Tbsp. chopped parsley
salt and pepper to taste

Preheat oven to 350°. Sauté onions and mushrooms in butter over medium heat until soft. Add remaining ingredients and continue cooking 2 minutes. Remove to a bowl.

**Step Two:**

1/2 lb. spinach, rinsed
2 Tbsp. butter
1 clove garlic, minced
1/4 cup whipping cream
salt and pepper to taste

Parboil spinach until tender; drain well. Pat dry with paper towels. Sauté garlic and spinach in butter over medium heat, tossing lightly. Add cream and seasonings. In food processor, puree until smooth.

**Step Three:**

3 Tbsp. butter
1/4 cup flour
1 cup milk
1 1/2 cups half-and-half
dash nutmeg
salt and pepper to taste
1 bay leaf
1/4 cup finely chopped onions
1 carrot, finely chopped
1 stalk celery, finely chopped

In saucepan over medium heat, melt butter and whisk in flour. Continue to whisk until flour is light brown. Meanwhile, blend milk and half-and-half in another saucepan and bring to a simmer. Turn heat under flour to low and whisk in milk mixture until smooth. Add remaining ingredients, cover, and set aside.

**Step Four:**

1 lb. fresh crabmeat, rinsed
juice from 1/2 lemon
2 Tbsp. freshly chopped parsley
2 Tbsp. freshly chopped basil
1/2 pkg. lasagna, cooked
4 oz. Parmesan cheese, freshly grated
1 8-oz. can tomato sauce

Toss crabmeat, lemon juice, parsley, and basil together in a bowl. In 7" x 12" baking dish, layer noodles, sauce from Step Three, Parmesan, mushrooms, and crabmeat. Top with more noodles, sauce, spinach, Parmesan, and sauce. Add final layers of noodles, crabmeat, Parmesan, sauce, tomato sauce, and more Parmesan. Bake 40 minutes uncovered.

# SUGGESTED MENU

Popping the Cork

## Gruyère Cheese Puffs

Riesling to the Occasion

## Avocados Stuffed with Tomatoes, Feta, and Chives

Zin Now . . . Play Later

## ♥Over a Barrel

Peel Me a Grape

## Acorn Squash with Bacon

Forbidden Fruit

## Chardonnay

# ♥ Message in a Bottle

*Let's cast away our inhibitions and pretend we're on a deserted isle!*

(marinate 1 hour)

Caribbean Grilled Shrimp with Banana-Rum Relish

**Step One:**

1/4 cup freshly squeezed lime juice

1 cup freshly squeezed orange,
   pineapple, guava, or tangerine juice
   (or a mixture)

1/4 cup rum

2 Tbsp. freshly chopped cilantro

1 tsp. apple cider vinegar

1 clove garlic, minced

1 lb. large shrimp, butterflied

Combine marinade ingredients in medium bowl. Add shrimp and marinate for 1 hour.

**Step Two:**

1 1/2 cup rice

Cook rice according to package directions.

**Step Three:**

1 Tbsp. butter

1 small clove garlic, minced

2 Tbsp. freshly squeezed orange,
   pineapple, guava, or tangerine juice
   (or a mixture)

1 Tbsp. freshly squeezed lime juice

2 Tbsp. rum

2 ripe bananas, chopped

1 Tbsp. freshly chopped cilantro

1 Tbsp. freshly minced chives

Melt butter in frying pan and add garlic; sauté until soft. Add juices, rum, and bananas; cook until bananas are heated through, about 3 minutes. Stir in cilantro and chives.

**Step Four:**

2–3 leaves red leaf lettuce

Remove shrimp from marinade and thread onto skewers. Grill until pink, about 3–4 minutes total. Be careful not to overcook. Mound rice on one side of each warmed plate; place leaf opposite. Remove shrimp from skewers and arrange in center. Spoon relish onto leaf and onto shrimp.

# SUGGESTED MENU

Popping the Cork

## Gruyère Cheese Puffs

Riesling to the Occasion

## Basil-Scented Sweet Potato Soup

## Kiwi, Orange, and Cranberry Salad with Poppy Seed Dressing

Zin Now . . . Play Later

## ♥ Message in a Bottle

Peel Me a Grape

## Acorn Squash with Bacon

Forbidden Fruit

## Gewürztraminer

# Folie à Deux

*...a fantasy for two. The course of the evening is up to you!*

Ahi Tuna in Mustard Beurre Blanc

**Step One:**

1 1/2 lbs. Ahi Tuna fillets
1/4 cup light olive oil
2 Tbsp. freshly chopped herbs (e.g., basil, thyme, tarragon)

Place tuna in baking dish. Mix oil and herbs and drizzle over fillets. Marinate 5–8 hours in refrigerator.

**Step Two:**

1/2 cup Sauternes, Sauvignon Blanc, or other dry white wine
6–8 green onion tops, minced
3/4 cup whipping cream
1/4 cup butter, cut into pieces
juice from 1/4 lemon
1/2 Tbsp. Dijon mustard
1/2 Tbsp. light soy sauce
salt and freshly ground pepper to taste

In saucepan over high heat, bring wine and onion to a boil. When wine is reduced to about 2 Tbsp., add cream. Continue to boil until reduced to 2/3 cup. Turn heat to low and whisk in butter, one piece at a time, until melted. Add remaining ingredients and keep warm.

**Step Three:**

2 small Roma tomatoes, finely chopped
1 Tbsp. minced parsley

Preheat grill or broiler. Grill or broil fillets about 2 minutes per side or until slightly opaque, brushing periodically with marinade to keep moist. Remove to warm plates. Spoon sauce over Ahi, garnish with chopped tomatoes and a sprinkling of parsley, and serve.

# SUGGESTED MENU

Popping the Cork

## Artichoke Dip

Riesling to the Occasion

## Basil-Scented Sweet Potato Soup

## Tomato-Olive Salad with Cumin-Scented Dressing

Zin Now . . . Play Later

## Folie à Deux

Peel Me a Grape

## French White and Green Beans

Forbidden Fruit

## Gewürztraminer

# Ambrosial Nectar

*Bacchus and Eros made a deal. With this meal your fate is sealed!*

Italian Shellfish Stew

**Step One:**

1/2 cup butter
1 onion, finely chopped
2 cups finely sliced mushrooms
1 green bell pepper, chopped
2 ribs celery, chopped
3 cloves garlic, chopped
1 carrot, finely chopped
1 large tomato, chopped
6–8 fresh basil leaves, chopped
1 bay leaf
1 Tbsp. fresh thyme
1 Tbsp. freshly chopped parsley
1 tsp. paprika
1/4 tsp. chili powder
1/4 tsp. fennel seeds, crushed
pinch saffron
3 12-ounce bottles clam juice
1 cup Zinfandel or other dry red wine
1/2 cup dry Vermouth
2 14-oz. cans vegetable broth
1 8-oz. can tomato sauce
3 tsp. tomato paste
1 lb. sea bass

Sauté onion in butter over medium heat until soft; remove to large stockpot. Sauté mushrooms until they begin to brown. Add to stockpot. Sauté pepper, celery, garlic, and carrot until softened. Add to stockpot. Add herbs and remaining ingredients, stirring until well blended. Cook as few as 3 or as many as 6 hours over low heat.

**Step Two:**

8 mussels, scrubbed and debearded
8 clams, scrubbed
1 large cooked crab, cleaned and
    cracked into pieces
1/2 lb. large shrimp

Ten minutes before serving, add clams and mussels. Five minutes before serving, add crab and shrimp. Serve in large bowls with lemon wedges and crusty French bread.

Popping the Cork

# Gruyère Cheese Puffs

Riesling to the Occasion

# Avocados Stuffed with Tomatoes, Feta, and Chives

Zin Now . . . Play Later

# ♥Ambrosial Nectar

Peel Me a Grape

# Angel Hair Pasta in Herb-Wine Sauce

Forbidden Fruit

# Zinfandel

# Blanc Magic

*Will you do that voodoo that you do so well?*

Scallops with Kirsch and Tarragon

**Step One:**

1 lb. fresh ocean scallops
1/4 cup chicken stock
1/4 cup kirsch

Combine scallops, stock, and kirsch in saucepan. Cook over medium heat until scallops begin to lose their translucency, 3–5 minutes. Reserving the liquid, transfer scallops to warm plate and cover loosely.

**Step Two:**

3 Tbsp. butter
3 Tbsp. flour
1/2 cup whipping cream
1 Tbsp. kirsch
1/2 tsp. tarragon
salt and pepper to taste
1 large bunch of spinach, washed and
    stems removed

Melt butter in a large saucepan over medium heat. Whisk in flour, stirring constantly, for 2 minutes. Add reserved liquid and continue to whisk until mixture is smooth. Add cream and kirsch, whisking constantly until sauce thickens. Add tarragon, salt, and pepper. Divide spinach leaves onto au gratin dishes or dinner plates and spoon scallops onto leaves; top with sauce and serve immediately.

## SUGGESTED MENU

Popping the Cork

*Herbed Wine and Cheese Spread*

Riesling to the Occasion

*Kiwi, Orange, and Cranberry
Salad with Poppy Seed Dressing*

Zin Now . . . Play Later

*Blanc Magic*

Peel Me a Grape

*French White and Green Beans*

Forbidden Fruit

*Sauvignon Blanc*

 # Uncorked Passion

*Let's do the twist and uncork our passions!*

Hot and Steamy Clam Chowder

**Step One:**

4 strips lean bacon, chopped
1 onion, chopped
2 cups whole milk
2 cups half-and-half
1 8-oz. bottle clam juice
1/2 cup Chardonnay
3 medium potatoes, peeled and diced
1 16-oz. can corn, drained
3 Tbsp. minced fresh parsley
1 tsp. fines herbes
1/2 tsp. thyme
1/2 tsp. celery salt
1/8 tsp. white pepper

In stockpot over medium heat, sauté bacon and onion until bacon is crisp. Drain off fat. Add remaining ingredients. Turn heat to low and simmer until potatoes are tender, about 15 minutes.

**Step Two:**

2 10-oz. cans whole baby clams, undrained
salt and pepper to taste
2 small Roma tomatoes, chopped

Add clams and seasonings to stockpot and continue simmering until just heated through. Ladle into warm bowls, garnish with tomatoes, and serve with crusty French bread.

# SUGGESTED MENU

Popping the Cork

## Salmon-Caviar Rolls

Riesling to the Occasion

## Avocados Stuffed with Tomatoes, Feta, and Chives

Zin Now . . . Play Later

## ♥Uncorked Passion

Peel Me a Grape

## Julienne of Carrots and Parsnips with Rosemary

## Angel Hair Pasta in Herb-Wine Sauce

Forbidden Fruit

## Chardonnay

# Double Trouble

*A magnum of bubbly . . . and you!*

Scallop-Stuffed Trout in Dill Sauce

**Step One:**

1/2 cup whipping cream
1/2 cup clam juice
1/3 cup Vermouth
2 Tbsp. Sauternes or other dry white
    wine
1/4 cup finely chopped dill
1/2 onion, chopped
1 clove garlic, minced

Preheat oven to 350°. Combine all ingredients in saucepan. Turn heat to high and bring to a boil. Reduce heat to low and simmer 20 minutes.

**Step Two:**

1/3 cup sliced almonds
2 10–12 oz. trout, cleaned, skinned,
    and boned
1/4 lb. bay scallops

Toast almonds in small frying pan over low heat until lightly browned. Ladle a little dill sauce into a baking dish and lay trout on top. Fill cavity of trout with scallops. Sprinkle with almonds and bake 20 minutes.

**Step Three:**

1 Tbsp. lemon juice
2 Tbsp. butter
1 Tbsp. finely chopped dill
fresh dill sprigs

Transfer fish to warmed plates and keep warm in oven at low temperature with door ajar. Add enough dill sauce to baking dish to bring liquid to 2 cups. Place over high heat and boil until sauce is reduced and thickened. Whisk in lemon juice, butter, and dill. Ladle sauce over trout and garnish with dill sprigs.

# SUGGESTED MENU

Popping the Cork

## Salmon-Caviar Rolls

Riesling to the Occasion

## Woodsy Madeira-Mushroom Soup

## Kiwi, Orange, and Cranberry Salad with Poppy Seed Dressing

Zin Now . . . Play Later

## ♥Double Trouble

Peel Me a Grape

## Angel Hair Pasta in Herb-Wine Sauce

## Julienne of Carrots and Parsnips with Rosemary

Forbidden Fruit

## Champagne or Pinot Blanc

 *Zin Today*

*. . . repent tomorrow!*

Grilled Lamb in Zinfandel-Cranberry Sauce

**Step One:**

1 lb. lamb bones
1 carrot, chopped
1 rib celery, chopped
1 small onion, chopped
2 cloves garlic, minced
2 Tbsp. tomato paste
1/2 tsp. chervil
1/2 tsp. marjoram
1/4 tsp. rosemary, crushed
1/4 tsp. thyme
1/4 tsp. white pepper
1 bay leaf
1/4 cup Sauvignon Blanc or other dry
  white wine

Roast lamb bones at 425° for 20 minutes. Add carrot, celery, onion, and garlic and roast 20 minutes more. Place pan on stove top over medium heat; add herbs and wine. Scrape brown bits from pan bottom into wine. Cover bones with at least 2" water and simmer 2 hours. Remove bones, turn heat to high, and boil until liquid is reduced by half.

**Step Two:**

1 cup cranberry-raspberry juice
1 cup Zinfandel or other dry red wine
4 Tbsp. butter
2 lb. boneless lamb steaks
fresh parsley sprigs

Add juice and wine to stock and bring to a boil, boiling until liquid is reduced to 1 cup. Strain out vegetables and discard. Whisk in 1 tablespoon of butter at a time until sauce thickens slightly. Grill lamb 6–8 minutes per side for medium rare. Spoon sauce over lamb, garnish with parsley, and serve.

# SUGGESTED MENU

Popping the Cork

## *Herbed Wine and Cheese Spread*

Riesling to the Occasion

## *Kiwi, Orange, and Cranberry Salad with Poppy Seed Dressing*

Zin Now . . . Play Later

## *♥Zin Today*

Peel Me a Grape

## *Acorn Squash with Bacon*

Forbidden Fruit

## *Zinfandel*

# ♥ Ménage à Trois

**30 minutes**

*A loaf of bread, a jug of wine, and ewe . . . the perfect threesome!*

Lamb Chops in Herbed Béarnaise Sauce

**Step One:**

1 1/2 Tbsp. minced leeks
1 small clove garlic, minced
2 Tbsp. freshly squeezed lemon juice
1/4 cup Sauternes or other dry white
    wine
1 Tbsp. tarragon
1/2 tsp. chervil
salt and pepper to taste

Combine ingredients in small saucepan over medium heat. Bring to a boil and boil until only 2 tablespoons remain, forming a glaze.

**Step Two:**

3 large egg yolks
1/8 tsp. cayenne
1/2 cup butter, melted

In blender or food processor, blend egg yolks and cayenne on high 10–15 seconds. Add glaze and let blender run on high while adding melted butter in a slow, steady stream through the hole in the top of the appliance. Replace lid and run on high 1 minute; let sit 30 seconds. Repeat until sauce thickens. Place blender jar in pot of warm water while grilling chops.

**Step Three:**

3–4 tenderloin chops, 1" to 1 1/2"
    thick, boned and well trimmed
salt and pepper to taste
2 Tbsp. snipped chives

Preheat broiler and season chops on both sides. Broil 3 1/2" from heat, 5 minutes per side. Remove to warm plates. Spoon sauce over chops, sprinkle with chives, and serve.

*58*

# SUGGESTED MENU

Popping the Cork

## *Phyllo Stuffed with Spinach and Cheese*

Riesling to the Occasion

## *Woodsy Madeira-Mushroom Soup*

## *Kiwi, Orange, and Cranberry Salad with Poppy Seed Dressing*

Zin Now . . . Play Later

## *♥Ménage à Trois*

Peel Me a Grape

## *French White and Green Beans*

Forbidden Fruit

## *Pinot Noir*

59

# *Unquenchable Me*

*I thirst for your love.*

Linguine, Prosciutto, and Baby Peas in Light Garlic Sauce

**Step One:**

3/4 lb. linguine

Bring stockpot of water to a boil; add pasta and cook until al dente. Drain.

**Step Two:**

2 Tbsp. butter
3/4 cup whipping cream
1 cup freshly grated Parmesan cheese
1 clove garlic, minced
1 Tbsp. freshly minced basil
1/2 cup frozen petite peas, thawed
2 thin slices prosciutto, chopped
parsley sprigs

Melt butter in small saucepan and toss with pasta. Stir in cream, cheese, garlic, basil, peas, and prosciutto. Serve on a warm plate garnished with parsley.

# SUGGESTED MENU

Popping the Cork

## Phyllo Stuffed with Spinach and Cheese

Riesling to the Occasion

## Basil-Scented Sweet Potato Soup

## Tomato-Olive Salad with Cumin-Scented Dressing

Zin Now . . . Play Later

## Unquenchable Me

Peel Me a Grape

## Julienne of Carrots and Parsnips with Rosemary

Forbidden Fruit

## Sauvignon Blanc

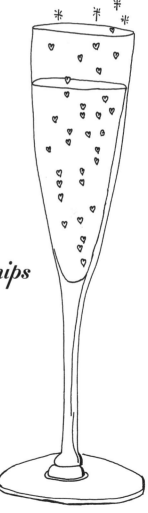

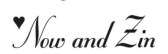

# Now and Zin

*. . . I vant to be alone with you!*

Pasta with Spicy Pesto, Peppers, and Sausages

**Step One:**

1/2 cup fresh parsley
1/2 cup fresh basil leaves
2 cloves garlic
2 Tbsp. light olive oil
2 Tbsp. freshly grated Parmesan cheese
1/4 tsp. freshly ground pepper
salt to taste

In food processor, chop basil and parsley until very fine. Add remaining ingredients and process until just blended, making a course pesto. Set aside.

**Step Two:**

1 lb. mild Italian sausage
1 green bell pepper, coarsely chopped
1 yellow bell pepper, coarsely chopped
1 red bell pepper, coarsely chopped
4 Roma tomatoes, chopped
1 onion, chopped
6–8 brown mushrooms, sliced
2 Tbsp. Chenin Blanc or other dry white wine

Remove sausage from casings. In frying pan over medium heat, fry sausage until done. Drain on paper towels and discard excess oil from pan. Sauté remaining vegetables and wine in frying pan until crisp-tender. Return sausage to pan and set aside.

**Step Three:**

3/4 lb. fettuccine or linguine

Cook pasta according to package directions until al dente; drain. In warm serving bowl, toss pasta with pesto sauce. Spoon sausage mixture over pasta and serve.

Popping the Cork

### Artichoke Dip

Riesling to the Occasion

### Avocados Stuffed with Tomatoes, Feta, and Chives

Zin Now . . . Play Later

### ♥Now and Zin

Peel Me a Grape

### Cauliflower in Creamy Basil Sauce

Forbidden Fruit

### Zinfandel

# A Wink and a Drink

*. . . can lead to more than you think!*

Pasta with Shrimp in Chive-Garlic Butter

**Step One:**

3/4 lb. pasta (linguine, fettuccine,
or spaghettini)

Cook pasta until al dente, beginning Step Two in the meantime. Drain well and transfer to a warm bowl.

**Step Two:**

5 Tbsp. butter, room temperature
3/4 lb. shrimp
3/4 cup chopped parsley
1 clove garlic, minced
3 Tbsp. snipped chives or 3 green
onions, minced
1 tsp. brandy
1/4 tsp. white pepper

Melt butter in frying pan over medium heat. Sauté shrimp until just pink. Stir in remaining ingredients. Toss shrimp and garlic butter with hot pasta; serve on warm plates with crusty French bread.

# SUGGESTED MENU

Popping the Cork

## Salmon-Caviar Rolls

Riesling to the Occasion

## Woodsy Madeira-Mushroom Soup

## Kiwi, Orange, and Cranberry Salad with Poppy Seed Dressing

Zin Now . . . Play Later

## ♥A Wink and a Drink

Peel Me a Grape

## Gratin of Spinach, Zucchini, and Herbs

Forbidden Fruit

## Chardonnay

# Rhône Rendezvous

1 hour, 45 minutes

*A tryst with taste!*

Savory Mushroom-Spinach Lasagne

**Step One:**

1 Tbsp. cooking oil
10–12 uncooked lasagna

Cook noodles according to package directions. Drain. Return to stockpot and cover with warm water.

**Step Two:**

1 Tbsp. olive oil
1 onion, finely chopped
1 clove garlic, minced
1 lb. brown mushrooms, sliced
1/4 cup Burgundy or other dry red wine

In large frying pan over medium heat, sauté onion and garlic in oil until soft. Add one batch of mushrooms, sauté until soft, and remove to a bowl. Repeat until all mushrooms are done. Return mushrooms to pan and add wine. Continue to sauté until almost all moisture evaporates.

**Step Three:**

1 lb. carrots, peeled and grated
1 14-oz. can sliced black olives
2 8-oz. cans tomato sauce
1 6-oz. can tomato paste
1 Tbsp. minced orange peel
1 tsp. oregano
1 tsp. basil
1 tsp. savory
1 tsp. sugar
1/2 tsp. salt
1/4 tsp. freshly ground pepper

Add carrots to pan, stirring, and cook 5 minutes. Add remaining ingredients; combine well and remove from heat. Preheat oven to 375°.

**Step Four:**

2 cups cottage cheese, well drained
2 lbs. fresh spinach, cooked and well drained
1 1/2 lbs. Monterey Jack cheese, grated
1/4 cup freshly grated Parmesan cheese

Grease 9" x 13" baking pan. Line with single layer of noodles. Top with half the cottage cheese, half the spinach, a third of the Monterey Jack, and half the tomato-olive mixture from Step Three. Repeat. Top lasagne with Monterey Jack and a sprinkling of Parmesan. Bake 45 minutes uncovered.

# SUGGESTED MENU

Popping the Cork

*Gruyère Cheese Puffs*

Riesling to the Occasion

*Avocados Stuffed with Tomatoes, Feta, and Chives*

Zin Now . . . Play Later

*Rhône Rendezvous*

Peel Me a Grape

*Cauliflower in Creamy Basil Sauce*

Forbidden Fruit

*Barbera*

# ♥ Château Libido

*Let's go incognito!*

Fettuccine in Salmon-Basil Sauce

### Step One:
2 Tbsp. butter
8 oz. fresh salmon, boned and cut
  into 3/4"dice
1 small onion, minced
1 tomato, chopped
1/4 cup bottled clam juice
1/4 cup Sauternes or other dry white
  wine

Melt butter in frying pan over medium heat. Add salmon and sauté until opaque, 30–45 seconds; transfer to a bowl. Add onion and tomato to pan and sauté until soft. Add clam juice and wine; turn heat to high and boil until syrupy. Remove pan from heat.

### Step Two:
3/4 lb. fettuccine
1 Tbsp. butter

Cook fettuccine according to package directions until al dente. Drain and move to warmed pasta bowl. Toss with butter.

### Step Three:
1/2 cup whipping cream
3 Tbsp. finely chopped fresh basil
3 oz. thinly sliced smoked salmon, cut
  into narrow ribbons
1 Tbsp. minced fresh parsley
salt and freshly ground pepper to taste

Add cream and basil to frying pan. Bring heat to high and boil until sauce thickens slightly. Gently fold in sautéed salmon. Turn heat to low. Fold in smoked salmon, parsley, pepper, and salt. Pour sauce over pasta and toss gently; serve with crusty French bread.

# SUGGESTED MENU

Popping the Cork

## Herbed Wine and Cheese Spread

Riesling to the Occasion

## Woodsy Madeira–Mushroom Soup

Zin Now . . . Play Later

## ♥Château Libido

Peel Me a Grape

## Gratin of Spinach, Zucchini, and Herbs

Forbidden Fruit

## Chardonnay

 **First Crush**

*You make me blush!*

Pork Chops in Black Cherry–Brandy Sauce

**Step One:**

2 large pork loin filets, 1" thick
salt and pepper to taste
2 Tbsp. butter
1 Tbsp. cooking oil
1 small onion, chopped
1/2 cup chicken broth
3/4 cup Port wine
1/4 cup kirsch

Season pork. Melt butter and heat oil in frying pan over medium heat. Add filets and brown lightly on both sides. Add onion; cook until tender. Drain off excess oil. Add stock, Port, and kirsch; cover and simmer over low heat for 1 hour.

**Step Two:**

1/2 lemon
1 apple, cored, peeled, and sliced
1 cup black cherries, pitted and halved

Squeeze lemon over apple. Add fruit to frying pan and simmer 5 additional minutes. Transfer filets to warm au gratin plates; cover and keep warm. Remove several cherries and apple slices and arrange on chops. Strain cooking liquid and remaining fruit through colander, breaking fruit up by pushing it through with a spoon. Return all to pan.

**Step Three:**

1/4 cup heavy cream

Turn heat to high and whisk cream into pan with stock and fruit. Continue to whisk until sauce thickens. Spoon sauce over pork and fruit and serve.

# SUGGESTED MENU

Popping the Cork

*Herbed Wine and Cheese Spread*

Riesling to the Occasion

*Woodsy Madeira-Mushroom Soup*

Zin Now . . . Play Later

*First Crush*

Peel Me a Grape

*Gratin of Spinach, Zucchini, and Herbs*

Forbidden Fruit

*Gamay Beaujolais*

# ♥ Gamay Getaway

*Forget the map, grab the wine!*

## Pork Chops in Tangy Mustard-Wine Sauce

**Step One:**

2–4 pork rib or loin chops
salt and pepper to taste
2 Tbsp. vegetable oil

Season chops with salt and pepper. Heat oil in frying pan over medium heat; add chops and brown on all sides. Remove to plate and keep warm.

**Step Two:**

1 onion, finely chopped
1 Tbsp. butter
1 1/4 cups dry white wine (e.g.,
   Sauternes or other dry white wine)
1 3/4 cups chicken stock

Add butter to pan and sauté onion until golden. Add wine and boil until liquid is reduced by half. Add stock. Return pork chops to pan. Cover and simmer 45 minutes. Transfer chops to plate and keep warm. Boil sauce until reduced to 2 cups. Turn heat to medium.

**Step Three:**

1/4 cup Dijon mustard
1 tsp. cornstarch ·
1 Tbsp. butter
2 Tbsp. minced parsley

In small bowl, whisk mustard and 1/4 cup sauce from Step Two until smooth; add to frying pan. In another bowl, blend cornstarch and 1 Tbsp. cold water until smooth; whisk into sauce until it thickens. Add butter and parsley and return pork to pan, turning to coat. Heat through. Serve.

## SUGGESTED MENU

Popping the Cork

*Gruyère Cheese Puffs*

Riesling to the Occasion

*Tomato-Olive Salad with
Cumin-Scented Dressing*

Zin Now . . . Play Later

♥ *Gamay Getaway*

Peel Me a Grape

*Acorn Squash with Bacon*

Forbidden Fruit

*Gamay Beaujolais*

# Lip Service

*Let's sip into something more comfortable!*

## Pork Chops and Apples in Flamed Calvados Cream Sauce

**Step One:**

1 Tbsp. butter

1 large apple, peeled, cored, and cut
    into rings 1/2" thick

2 Tbsp. Calvados

Melt butter in frying pan over medium heat. Add apples, turning to coat. Sauté 3–4 minutes, or until firm and golden. Add Calvados to pan; heat 20–30 seconds and ignite. Turn heat to low and shake pan until flames die. Remove apples to dish and set pan aside, reserving liquid.

**Step Two:**

1 Tbsp. vegetable oil

2 boneless pork loin chops, 1 1/2"
    thick and well trimmed

2 Tbsp. Calvados

1/3 cup apple cider

1/4 tsp. sage

1/4 tsp. thyme

1/4 tsp. marjoram

freshly ground pepper

In separate frying pan, heat oil over medium heat. Add chops and brown well on both sides, about 5 minutes per side. Pour off any excess oil. Add Calvados; turn heat to low and ignite. When flames die, add cider and seasonings; cover and simmer 30 minutes.

**Step Three:**

Preheat broiler. Remove chops to au gratin or ovenproof dish and top with apples. Add liquid from Step One to frying pan. Turn heat to high and boil until reduced to a syrup. Brush syrup over apples and broil chops and fruit 2–3 minutes.

**Step Four:**

1/2 cup whipping cream

Whisk cream into remaining syrup. Turn heat to high and boil until sauce thickens. Spoon over chops and serve.

# SUGGESTED MENU

Popping the Cork

## Phyllo Stuffed with Spinach and Cheese

Riesling to the Occasion

## Kiwi, Orange, and Cranberry Salad with Poppy Seed Dressing

Zin Now . . . Play Later

## ♥Lip Service

Peel Me a Grape

## Julienne of Carrots and Parsnips with Rosemary

Forbidden Fruit

## Pinot Noir

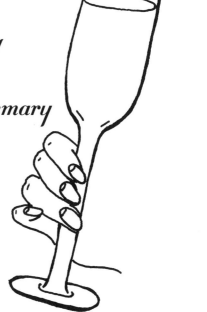

# ♥ A Little Bubbly

*...might get us into troubly. Oh, let's have a lot!*

**1 hour, 30 minutes**

(marinate 3–4 hours)

Marinated Prawn and Angel Hair Pasta Salad

**Step One:**

1 bunch green onions, finely chopped
2 Tbsp. butter
1/2 cup Sauternes
1 lb. medium-size prawns

In butter over medium heat, sauté onions until softened. Add wine and continue to cook until almost all the liquid is gone and what remains is syrupy. Add prawns and cook until pink on all sides. Remove all to a bowl.

**Step Two:**

1/4 cup light olive oil
1/4 cup Sauternes
1 tsp. thyme
2 Tbsp. minced parsley

Mix ingredients together and pour over prawns. Refrigerate 3–4 hours.

**Step Three:**

1 bunch green onions, finely chopped
2 Tbsp. butter
1/2 cup Sauternes

Sauté onions in butter over medium heat until softened. Add wine and continue to cook until almost all the liquid is gone and remainder is syrupy.

**Step Four:**

1/4 cup light olive oil
1/4 cup Sauternes
1 tsp. thyme
2 Tbsp. minced parsley
2 tsp. lemon zest
3/4 lb. angel hair pasta
parsley sprigs

Add all ingredients except pasta to syrup, blending well to make dressing. Cook pasta until al dente, rinse in cold water, and toss with dressing. Refrigerate until prawns are ready. Top pasta with prawns, garnish with sprigs of fresh parsley, and serve.

# SUGGESTED MENU

Popping the Cork

## Artichoke Dip

Riesling to the Occasion

## Woodsy Madeira-Mushroom Soup

Zin Now . . . Play Later

## A Little Bubbly

Peel Me a Grape

## French White and Green Beans

Forbidden Fruit

## Champagne or Sauvignon Blanc

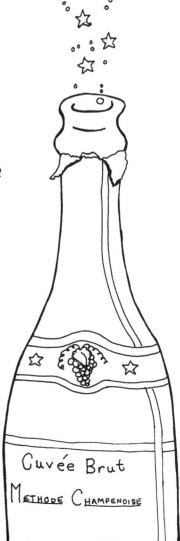

77

# ♥ In the "Oui" Hours

*The party's over, but the night is still young!*

Tortellini-Zucchini Salad with Dijon Vinaigrette

**Step One:**

1 tsp. Dijon mustard
2 Tbsp. red wine vinegar
1/4 cup light olive oil

Whisk mustard and vinegar together in small bowl. Add oil slowly, whisking continuously, until well blended.

**Step Two:**

1/2 zucchini

Using a fork, score zucchini lengthwise. Slice into 1/4" slices. Bring a pan of water to boil; add zucchini and parboil 1 minute. Remove with slotted spoon and plunge into bowl of ice water. Drain and reserve.

**Step Three:**

1 lb. fresh tortellini
2 Tbsp. minced parsley
3 Tbsp. freshly grated Parmesan cheese
1/2 lb. butter leaf lettuce, washed and
   torn into bite-size pieces

Cook tortellini in boiling water until al dente. Drain and combine with zucchini, three-quarters of dressing, parsley, and Parmesan. Toss greens with remaining dressing and arrange on plates. Top with pasta and serve.

# SUGGESTED MENU

Popping the Cork

*Herbed Wine and Cheese Spread*

Riesling to the Occasion

*Basil-Scented Sweet Potato Soup*

Zin Now . . . Play Later

*♥In the "Oui" Hours*

Peel Me a Grape

*Cauliflower in Creamy Basil Sauce*

Forbidden Fruit

*Pinot Grigio*

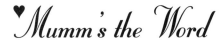

# Mumm's the Word

*Don't kiss and tell!*

Chilled Caper, Dill, Salmon, and Linguine Salad

**Step One:**

3/4 lb. linguine
1 Tbsp. light olive oil

Cook linguine according to package directions. Drain, rinse with cold water, and transfer to a chilled pasta bowl. Toss with oil.

**Step Two:**

1 Tbsp. finely chopped fresh dill
1 Tbsp. finely chopped red onion
1 Tbsp. capers, rinsed
1 Tbsp. light olive oil
8 oz. thinly sliced smoked salmon,
   cut into 1/2" x 1/2" pieces

Gently combine all ingredients with pasta and chill.

**Step Three:**

2 Tbsp. Sauvignon Blanc or other dry
   white wine
2 Tbsp. lemon juice
1 tsp. Dijon mustard
1/4 cup light olive oil

In small bowl, whisk wine, lemon juice, and mustard until well blended. Add oil, whisking constantly until very well blended. Toss with pasta and serve.

# SHHHHH....

Popping the Cork

*Artichoke Dip*

Riesling to the Occasion

*Woodsy Madeira–Mushroom Soup*

Zin Now . . . Play Later

*♥Mumm's the Word*

Peel Me a Grape

*Gratin of Spinach, Zucchini, and Herbs*

Forbidden Fruit

*Sparkling Wine or Sauvignon Blanc*

# Acorn Squash with Bacon

**1 hour, 15 minutes**

**Step One:**

3 slices bacon
1 acorn squash, halved and seeded
2 Tbsp. brown sugar
salt and pepper to taste
3 Tbsp. butter

Preheat oven to 350°. Lay bacon in large baking dish and bake for 15 minutes. Drain on paper towels. Place squash, cut side down, in baking dish; bake 1 hour. Transfer squash to heated platter and sprinkle with sugar, salt, and pepper. Dot with butter and crumble bacon over top.

# Julienne of Carrots and Parsnips with Rosemary

**45 minutes**

**Step One:**

4 carrots, peeled
4 parsnips, peeled

Cut carrots and parsnips into pieces 2" in length, then into thin, matchstick-size strips.

**Step Two:**

1 14-oz. can low-salt chicken stock
3 Tbsp. butter
1 Tbsp. fresh rosemary, minced
salt and freshly ground pepper to taste

In saucepan over medium heat, bring stock to a boil. Add carrots and cook until just tender; use a slotted spoon to remove to a bowl. Repeat with parsnips. Turn heat to high and boil stock until reduced to 1/4 cup. Whisk in butter, stir in rosemary, and season with salt and pepper. Return vegetables to pan and heat through.

# Cauliflower in Creamy Basil Sauce  20 minutes

**Step One:**

1/2 head cauliflower, broken into florets

Steam cauliflower until tender.

**Step Two:**

1 Tbsp. butter
2 Tbsp. whipping cream
1/8 tsp. cayenne
1 Tbsp. freshly minced basil

Melt butter in frying pan over medium heat. Whisk in cream; add cayenne and basil. Pour over cauliflower and serve immediately.

# Angel Hair Pasta in Herb-Wine Sauce  45 minutes

**Step One:**

1/2 cup Sauternes or other dry white wine
4 Tbsp. butter
1 cup whipping cream
1/2 tsp. salt
1/8 tsp. freshly grated nutmeg
pinch of cayenne

In saucepan over medium heat, bring wine to a boil and boil until reduced by half. Whisk in butter. Add remaining ingredients and simmer 10 minutes or until slightly thickened. Meanwhile, begin Step Two.

**Step Two:**

1/2 lb. pasta, angel hair or spaghettini

Cook pasta according to package directions until al dente. Drain and transfer to warm serving bowl.

**Step Three:**

1/4 cup Parmesan cheese
1/4 cup freshly minced basil
1/4 cup freshly minced parsley
2 tsp. marjoram
salt and freshly ground pepper to taste

Turn heat under sauce to low; whisk in cheese and herbs. Season with salt and pepper. Gently toss with pasta and serve.

# Gratin of Spinach, Zucchini, and Herbs

**1 hour, 45 minutes**

**Step One:**

1 1/2 lbs. fresh spinach, rinsed

Preheat oven to 375°. Steam spinach until wilted; drain well and set aside.

**Step Two:**

2 Tbsp. light olive oil
1 small Vidalia or Maui onion, minced
4 cloves garlic, minced
2 medium zucchini, chopped

Sauté onion and garlic in oil over medium heat until soft. Add zucchini and continue to cook until zucchini is crisp-tender.

**Step Three:**

1/2 cup half-and-half
3 eggs
2 Tbsp. orange peel, minced
1 Tbsp. finely chopped fresh basil
1 Tbsp. finely chopped fresh thyme
1 tsp. freshly ground pepper
1 tsp. salt
1/2 cup grated Monterey Jack cheese
1/2 cup grated mozzarella cheese

Combine spinach, zucchini, half-and-half, eggs, and seasonings in food processor or blender. Puree until smooth. Pour into a bowl and fold in cheese until well combined. Transfer to greased casserole or baking pan.

**Step Four:**

1 Tbsp. butter, melted
1 cup day-old bread crumbs
1/2 tsp. seasoned salt
1 Tbsp. minced parsley

Combine ingredients in bowl, tossing until well combined. Spread over spinach and zucchini mixture and bake 35–40 minutes, until firm to the touch.

# French White and Green Beans

**Step One:**

1/4 lb. young string beans, trimmed
1/2 tsp. salt

Fill a saucepan halfway with water; add salt and bring to a boil. Add beans and cook, uncovered, until crisp-tender.

**Step Two:**

1 clove garlic, minced
2 Tbsp. light olive oil
1/4 tsp. thyme
1/4 cup Sauternes or other dry white
    wine
1 14-oz. can small white beans, drained
salt and freshly ground pepper to taste

In large saucepan over medium heat, slowly cook garlic in oil until golden. Remove garlic. Add thyme, wine, and white beans; cover and continue to cook over low heat for 5 minutes. Add string beans. Season with salt and pepper and continue to cook until heated through. Serve.

# SUBJECT INDEX

## Lamb

## Pasta

# RECIPE INDEX

# AS YOU LIKE IT
(Notes)

# *AS YOU LIKE IT*
(Notes)

# AS YOU LIKE IT

(Notes)